Glam Wedding FAVORS

To help your wedding guests remember the elegance of your special day, present them with little gifts that sparkle and shine. The DIY favors in this book are all easy projects that are inexpensive ways to present delicious candies, cookies, candles, cake pops, miniature drinks, and other treats.

LEISURE ARTS, INC. • Maumelle, Arkansas

Treat Box

SHOPPING LIST

For each treat box:

- ☐ Wilton® 2" x 2" x 2" glittery favor box
- ☐ dimensional pearl and gem cluster sticker (Ours is from Jolee's Boutique®.)
- ☐ 10" of 3/4"w ribbon
- ☐ mints, candy, nuts or other desired treat
- ☐ hot glue gun and glue sticks

To make the Box:

1. Assemble the box. Fill the box with desired treat and close.
2. Knot the ribbon around the box; trim the ends as desired.
3. Use hot glue to adhere the sticker to the knot.

Wrapped Candy Favor

SHOPPING LIST

For each candy bar:

- ☐ candy bar with gold foil inner liner (We used a 3.5 oz. bar.)
- ☐ scrapbook paper
- ☐ $4^{3}/_{4}$" diameter paper doily
- ☐ rubber stamp (Ours says "Thank You.")
- ☐ gold metallic pigment-based ink pad
- ☐ double-sided tape

To make the Candy Favor:

1. Cut the scrapbook paper to wrap around the candy bar and overlap and slightly shorter than the length of the bar. Wrap the paper around the bar and secure on the back with the double-sided tape.
2. Use the stamp and ink to add the words to the paper doily. Use double-sided tape to secure the doily on the candy bar front.

Bubble Vial

SHOPPING LIST

For each bubble vial:

- ☐ clear celebration bubble tube
- ☐ clear bead cluster floral pick
- ☐ silver glitter cardstock
- ☐ 7" length of ribbon
- ☐ silver extra-fine glitter
- ☐ 1/4" hole punch
- ☐ wire cutters
- ☐ tracing paper

To make the Bubble Vial:

1. Shake a small amount of glitter into the bubble tube; close securely.
2. Cut apart the bead pick to include 3 beads with wire stems. Twist the wire stems together and around the top of the tube.
3. Trace the pattern, page 23, onto tracing paper; cut out. Use the pattern to cut a tag from the cardstock. Punch a hole in the square end.
4. Use the ribbon to tie the tag to the tube; trim the ribbon ends as desired.

Confetti Cones

SHOPPING LIST

For each confetti cone:

- ☐ $8^1/_2$" x 11" piece of printed vellum paper
- ☐ 18" of $^7/_8$"w sheer ribbon
- ☐ clear rhinestone cluster floral pick
- ☐ $^3/_4$" diameter clear round acrylic stone
- ☐ $^1/_4$" hole punch
- ☐ clear tape
- ☐ hot glue gun and glue sticks
- ☐ eco-friendly confetti

To make the Cone:

1. Roll the paper into a cone shape; tape.
2. Punch two holes in the front of cone.
3. Thread the ribbon through the holes and tie into a bow.
4. Cut the floral pick into three pieces with three stones each. Twist the wire stems together. Insert the wire ends through one of the holes and hot glue the ends inside. Arrange the rhinestone clusters.
5. Hot glue the stone to the bow.
6. Fill the cone with confetti.

Gold Glitter Fans

SHOPPING LIST

For each fan:

- ☐ gold glitter cardstock
- ☐ white cardstock
- ☐ computer and printer
- ☐ hot glue gun and glue sticks
- ☐ large wood craft sticks
- ☐ gold permanent pen
- ☐ gold metallic spray paint
- ☐ tracing paper

To make the Fan:

1. Paint the craft stick with the spray paint.
2. Use your computer to create a saying and to add the couple's names in the desired font and placed within an approximately 3" x 3 1/2" area; print onto the white cardstock.
3. Trace the patterns, pages 22 & 23) onto tracing paper; cut out. Use the patterns to cut the large fan and the heart from the gold glitter cardstock.
4. Centering the words, use the pattern to cut the small fan from the white cardstock.
5. Use the permanent pen to add dots around the edge of the sma fan. Glue the heart to the small fan.
6. Glue the small fan to the large fan. Glue the large fan to the craf stick.

Candy Basket

SHOPPING LIST

For each candy basket:

- ☐ glittered white scalloped-edge box
- ☐ gold glitter cardstock
- ☐ 1$\frac{1}{2}$"w heart-shaped punch
- ☐ 8mm pearl bead half
- ☐ 6" of $\frac{7}{8}$"w gold and white stiff ribbon for handle
- ☐ hot glue gun and glue sticks
- ☐ desired candy

To make the Basket:

1. Assemble the box.
2. Punch a heart from the cardstock.
3. Glue the heart to one side of the basket. Glue the pearl to the top of the heart.
4. Glue the ends of the ribbon to opposite sides inside the basket.
5. Place the candy in the basket.

Glittered Champagne Bottles

SHOPPING LIST

For each bottle:

- ☐ individual serving size bottles of champagne, sparkling apple juice, or sparkling grape juice
- ☐ gold glitter
- ☐ 18" of 7/8"w white sheer ribbon
- ☐ 8" of gold metallic cord
- ☐ white cardstock
- ☐ gold permanent pen
- ☐ spray adhesive
- ☐ painter's tape
- ☐ 1/8" hole punch
- ☐ newspaper
- ☐ tracing paper

To make the Bottle:

1. Cover the top of the bottle (foil portion, if applicable) with newspaper; tape along the bottom edge.
2. Spray the remainder of the bottle with spray adhesive.
3. Working over newspaper to catch the excess glitter, sprinkle glitter on the bottle.
4. Trace the pattern, page 23, onto tracing paper; cut out. Use the pattern to cut a tag from the cardstock. Punch a hole in the pointed end. Use the pen to write "Cheers!" on the tag.
5. Loosely tie the ribbon in a bow around the bottle; trim the ends as desired.
6. Use the cord to tie the tag to the ribbon.

Cheers!
Cheers!

Wine Glass Favor

SHOPPING LIST

For each glass:

- ☐ plastic wine glass
- ☐ gold spray paint
- ☐ black chalkboard tag
- ☐ 12" x 20" tissue paper sheet
- ☐ 18" length of gold metallic cord
- ☐ gold metallic permanent pen
- ☐ newspaper
- ☐ painter's tape
- ☐ desired candy

To make the Glass:

1. Cover the top of the glass with newspaper; tape the bottom edge to the stem.
2. Spray the stem and base of the glass with spray paint.
3. Use the permanent pen to write a sentiment on the tag.
4. Place the candy in the center of the tissue paper. Slide the tag on the gold cord. Gather the tissue paper together and tie with the gold cord. Trim the ends of the cord as desired.

to happiness
to happiness
to happiness

Cake Pop Station

SHOPPING LIST

For sign and each cake pop:

- ☐ wood frame with 4" x 6" opening and stand
- ☐ black glitter cardstock
- ☐ white cardstock
- ☐ 18" of $2^1/_2$"w wire-edge ribbon
- ☐ computer and printer
- ☐ hot glue gun and glue sticks
- ☐ craft knife
- ☐ tracing paper

To make the Cake Pop Station:

1. Fold the tracing paper in half. Trace the pattern, page 24, onto the tracing paper; cut out. Use the pattern to cut the frame from the cardstock. Center and glue the cardstock frame to the front of the wood frame.
2. Cutting from the back, use the craft knife to cut out the frame opening.
3. Tie the ribbon in a bow; glue the bow to the frame.
4. Use your computer and desired font to make a sign on white cardstock for your cake pop station, printing within a 3" x 5" area. Center and trim the sign to fit in the frame opening. Glue the printed cardstock to the back of the frame.

Personalize purchased cake pops with a rhinestone pop stick accented with a gold metallic bow.

Cookie Pillow Pouch

SHOPPING LIST

For each pouch:

- ☐ 3 1/2" x 5 1/4" clear pillow pouch
- ☐ 3 1/2" diameter paper doily
- ☐ 5/8"w gold glitter tape
- ☐ small gold metallic flower spray
- ☐ rubber stamp (Ours says "All You Need Is Love.")
- ☐ gold metallic pigment-based ink pad
- ☐ frosted glass finish spray paint
- ☐ craft glue
- ☐ plastic wrap
- ☐ cookie (Try our Favorite Chocolate Chip Cookie recipe, right.)

To make the Pouch:

1. Paint the outside of the pouch with frosted glass finish spray paint.
2. Cut the doily in half. Use the stamp and ink to add the words to the paper doily. Glue the upper edge of the doily on the lower half of the pouch front.
3. Place the glitter tape around the pouch over the top edge of the doily.
4. Glue the flower spray to the glitter tape.
5. Wrap the cookie in plastic wrap. Place the cookie in the pouch.

Favorite Chocolate Chip Cookies

1 cup butter, softened
1 cup granulated sugar
1 cup firmly packed brown sugar
2 eggs
1 teaspoon vanilla extract
2 cups all-purpose flour
1 teaspoon baking soda
1/2 teaspoon salt
2 cups old-fashioned oats
1 cup semisweet chocolate chips
1 cup chopped pecans

In a large bowl, cream butter, sugars, eggs, and vanilla until fluffy. In a separate bowl, combine flour, baking soda, and salt. Add to creamed mixture, mixing thoroughly.

Place oats in a blender or food processor and process until the texture of coarse meal. Stir oats into dough with chocolate chips and pecans. Cover and freeze 1 hour.

Shape dough into 1-inch balls and place on ungreased baking sheets. Bake at 375°F for 9 to 12 minutes or until lightly browned around the edges. Cool cookies slightly on baking sheets; transfer to wire racks to cool.

Yield: about 6 dozen cookies

Monogrammed Candy Jar

SHOPPING LIST

For each candy jar:

- ☐ small glass tilt jar with black lid (lid can be spray painted, if needed)
- ☐ self-adhesive rhinestone circle to fit lid
- ☐ black and rhinestone acrylic stone
- ☐ white glitter cardstock
- ☐ clear monogram stickers to fit side of jar
- ☐ circle punch to fit side of jar
- ☐ glue dots
- ☐ desired colorful candy

To make the Jar:

1. Fill the jar with candy. Place the lid on the jar.
2. Punch a circle from the cardstock.
3. Adhere the monogram sticker to the cardstock circle.
4. Use a glue dot to adhere the circle to the side of the jar.
5. Adhere the rhinestones to the lid.
6. Use a glue dot to adhere the stone to the lid.

Votive Candle Holders

SHOPPING LIST

For each votive:

- ☐ clear glass votive holder (Ours are about 1 1/2" diameter.)
- ☐ white votive candle
- ☐ 4mm gold, square, self-adhesive gemstones
- ☐ flat black spray paint
- ☐ black cardstock
- ☐ 1 1/2" diameter circle punch
- ☐ 1/8" hole punch
- ☐ 10" of 1/8"w gold metallic braid trim
- ☐ gold metallic cord
- ☐ heart design rubber stamp
- ☐ gold pigment-based ink pad
- ☐ 4" x 2" x 6" treat bag
- ☐ clear tape

1. Spray paint the votive holder black; insert the candle.
2. Adhere the gemstones around the top of the votive.
3. Punch a 1 1/2" circle from the cardstock.
4. Use stamp and ink to add the heart design to the paper circle. Punch a hole on one side of the circle.
5. Place the votive in the bag. Gather the top and tie a bow with the braid trim. Tape the corners of the bag under the votive holder.
6. Use the gold cord to tie the circle to the votive holder.

Crystal Key Chain

SHOPPING LIST

For each key chain:

- ☐ large clear faceted jewel stone
- ☐ 1 1/4" length of silver chain
- ☐ 2 assorted bead charms
- ☐ printed cardstock
- ☐ 9mm jump ring
- ☐ three 6mm jump rings
- ☐ 24mm split ring
- ☐ 10" of 7/8"w white sheer ribbon
- ☐ rubber stamps (initials and &)
- ☐ black pigment-based ink pad
- ☐ 2"w heart-shaped paper punch
- ☐ 1/4" hole punch
- ☐ chain-nose pliers (2 pair)

To make the Key Chain:

1. Use the large jump ring to attach the large jewel stone to one end of the chain.
2. Use small jump rings to attach the charms near the bottom of the chain as desired.
3. Use a small jump ring to attach the chain to the split ring.
4. Punch a heart from the cardstock.
5. Use the stamps and the ink to add the initials to the paper heart. Punch a hole on one side of the heart.
6. Slide the heart and split ring on the ribbon. Tie the ribbon in a bow; trim the ends as desired.

Opening and Closing Jump Rings

Hold one side of the jump ring with chain-nose pliers. With a second pair of chain-nose pliers, gently hold the other side of the jump ring. Open the jump ring by pulling one pair of pliers toward you while pushing the other away ***(Fig. 1)***.

Fig. 1

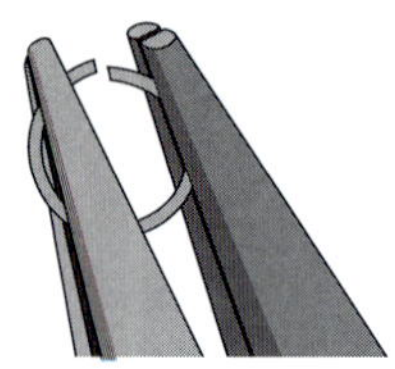

Close the jump ring by pushing and pulling the pliers in opposite directions, bringing the ring ends back together.

M&J

Love

Candy Jar

SHOPPING LIST

For each jar:

- ☐ small jar with lid (ours are approximately 2"w x $3^{1}/_{2}$"t)
- ☐ 18 8mm pearl beads
- ☐ crystal metal-lined bead
- ☐ 12" of $^{5}/_{8}$"w black and white print ribbon
- ☐ 30" of 20-gauge wire
- ☐ silver spray paint
- ☐ silver glitter
- ☐ black permanent pen
- ☐ spray adhesive
- ☐ painter's tape
- ☐ wire cutters
- ☐ pencil
- ☐ newspaper
- ☐ desired candy

To make the Jar:

1. Spray the lid with spray adhesive. Working over newspaper to catch the excess glitter, apply glitter to the lid.
2. Place tape around top and bottom of jar, leaving an area 1" high in the center uncovered.
3. Paint the uncovered area of the jar with the spray paint. When dry, use the pen to write a word on the jar.
4. Leaving 5" of wire at the end, loosely wrap the wire around the top of the jar; twist the wire together.
5. To make the handle, slide the pearls on the wire, bend the wire into a handle shape, and twist the end of the wire around itself on the opposite side of the jar. Leaving 5" of wire, trim the wire end.
6. Twist the ends of the wire around the pencil to coil; remove the pencil.
7. Knot the center of the ribbon length to the handle on one side of the jar.
8. Fold the ribbon into two loops. Slide the crystal bead on one loop and tail. Slide the bead close to the handle.
9. Fill the jar with candy. Replace the lid.

Patterns

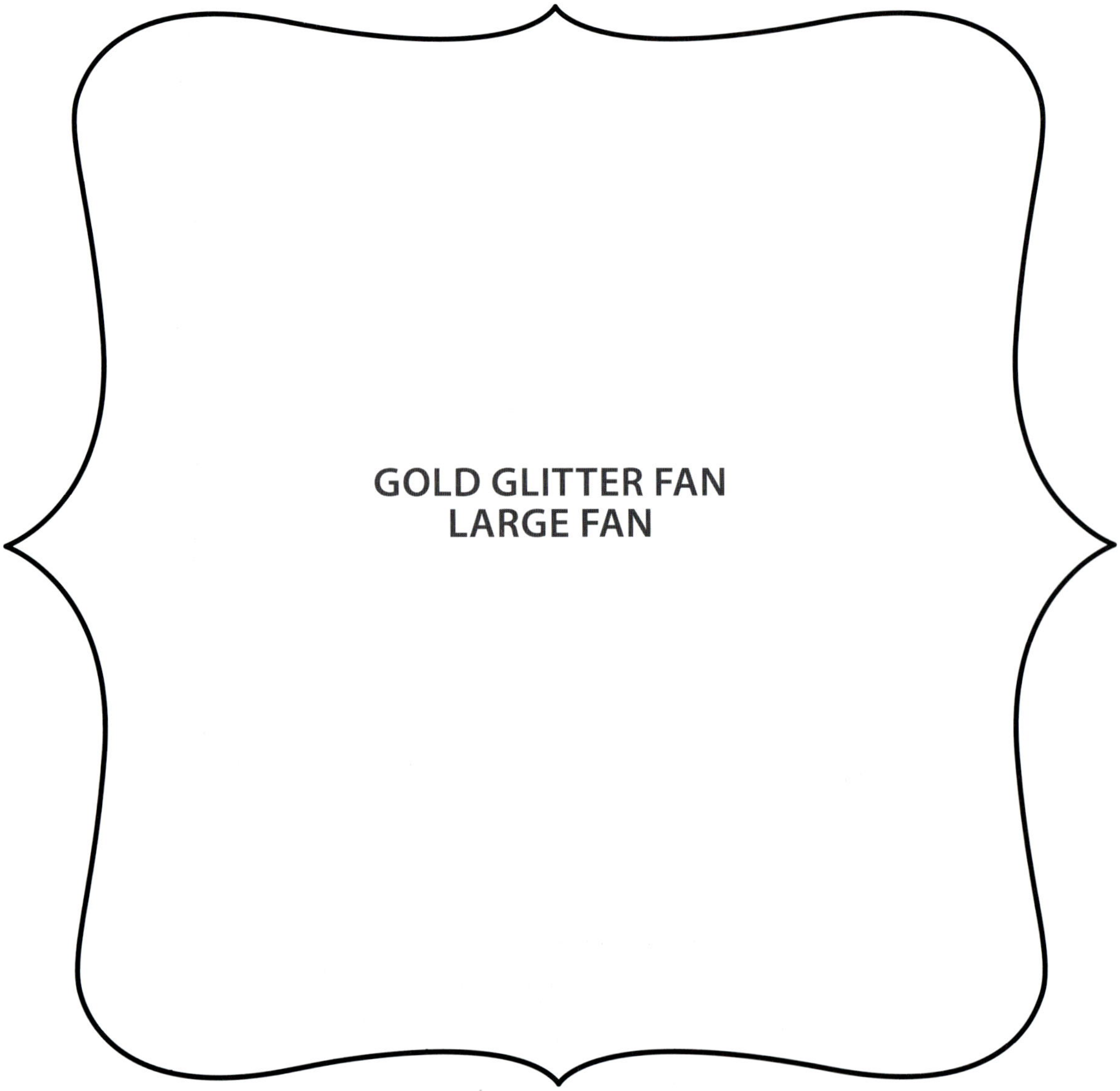

HEART PATTERN

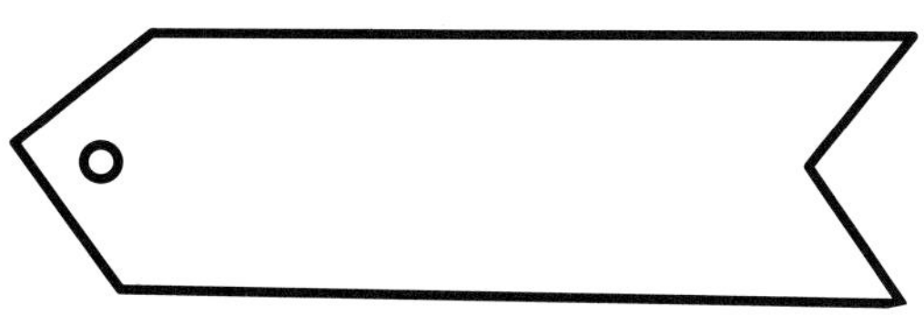

GLITTERED CHAMPAGNE
BOTTLE TAG

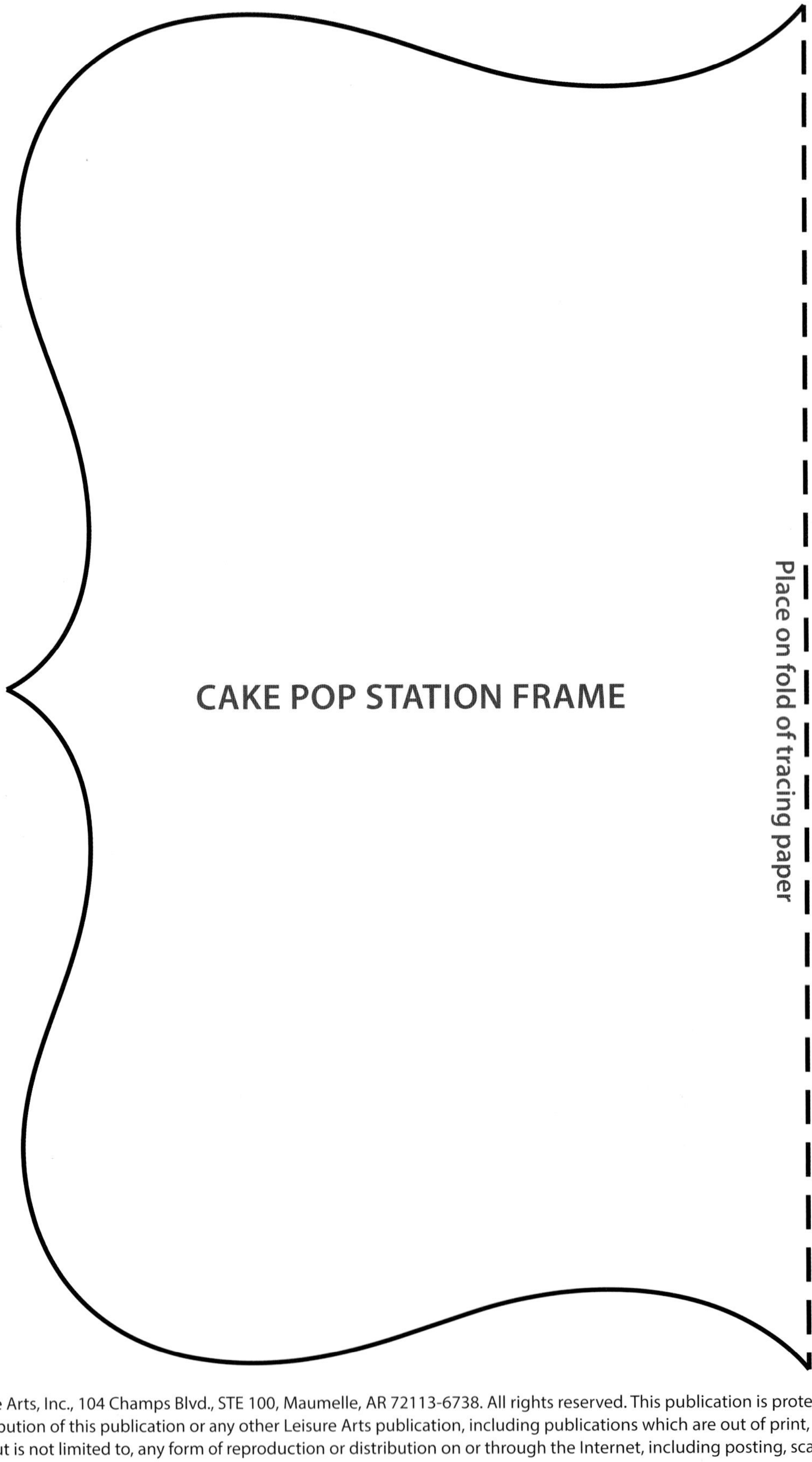

Production Team: Product Development Director - Anna L. Andrews; Designer - Kelly Reider; Contributing Designers - Kim Hamblin and Becky Werle; Technical Writer – Lisa Lancaster; Technical Associate – Mary Sullivan Hutcheson; Editorial Writer – Susan Frantz Wiles; Senior Graphic Artist – Lora Puls; Photostylist – Lori Wenger; Photographer – Jason Masters.